I DREAM OF MADONNA

<u>1st Dream</u> - August 1991

Madonna was a snake. Her head was on a snake's body. She was slithering around on my roof, which transformed into a wild jungle. There were various exotic animals scurrying through bushes and leaf clusters. I looked through the trees and saw my grandmother dancing around in my backyard. She was humming the tune, "Holiday". As she was dancing, she was tormenting a bird in a pine tree with a flute. She started to play the flute, she tried to play "Dear Jessie", but it sounded like a high-pitched screech. Madonna was slithering towards me, so I closed my...

Renee Bolgar

I have a Dream!...

TO: BVM
c/o GITN,
P.O. Box 49828,
Austin, Texas, 78765
U.S.A.

For U.S. addresses
F Flower
USA

madonna

Renee '91

I Dream of Madonna

WOMEN'S DREAMS OF THE GODDESS OF POP

Edited with an Introduction by
KAY TURNER

Original graphics by
DAVID KOLWYCK AND KAY TURNER

CollinsPublishersSanFrancisco

A Division of HarperCollins*Publishers*

THIS BOOK IS DEDICATED TO MADONNA
AND TO THE MADONNA IN YOU

On the cover: front, photograph by Bennett-Spooner, Gamma Liaison /
late 19th-century chromolithograph; back, details of photographs by
Oliviu Savu (left x 2) and Kent Loving, courtesy of Lauren Sommer (right);
background, photo Oliviu Savu / collage by Sheri Tornatore.

First Published in the USA in 1993 by
Collins Publishers San Francisco

Library of Congress Cataloging-in-Publication Data

Turner, Kay, 1948-
    I dream of Madonna : women's dreams of the
goddess of pop / edited by Kay Turner;
original graphics by Kay Turner and David Kolwyck.

        p.   cm.
    ISBN 0-00-255257-4
    1. Madonna, 1959- —— Influence. 2. Women's dreams. I. Title.
ML420.M1387T9 1993
782.42166'092—dc20   93-22592
                                          CIP

Printed in Slovenia

CONTENTS

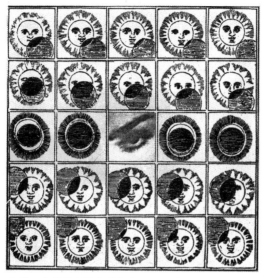

AN INVITATION TO DREAM

KAY TURNER

IN 1985 THE JUST-RISING STAR Madonna Ciccone was thought to be a new scourge on the feminist movement. She flaunted her sexiness and sang about being a virgin; she made outrageous claims about her ambitions, but invited the world to join her in believing that dreams come true. Her wilfulness looked like courage to some, contempt to others. Wannabes fiercely imitated her, but the standard feminist reaction was loathing laced with dread. Quoted in *Time* magazine in 1985, Madonna answered the assaults of feminists by saying, "To call me anti-feminist is ludicrous. Some people have said that I'm setting women back thirty years...Women aren't like men. They can do things that men can't do."

Despite negative criticism, Madonna consistently demonstrated that her position on women's difference is based in a confrontational style that explicitly challenges patriarchal ownership of women's sexuality. Madonna's position on women's difference was not set out as theory, but as practice. She eschewed the rhetoric of equality between the sexes in favor of a deliberately performed provocation, and began to promote women's sexual difference as seductive and healthy to women themselves. She was pro-choice in a way that asserted a woman's right to choose in all aspects of her life.

And although the media largely painted her as a conniving Machiavelli, Madonna repeatedly expressed that she worked from emotional impulses, fantasies, and unconscious creative sources. Like a (virgin) goddess, she gleefully released the contents of her own Pandora's Box, which among other things contained Aphrodite's love girdle refigured as a golden bustier, Artemis' bow transformed into a microphone, Athena's Gorgon shield revealed to be a Boy Toy belt, and the Virgin Mary's blue mantle translated into a black slip.

No other pop star of her prominence has so unabashedly and relentlessly promoted a woman-centered critique of female eroticism and its power. Madonna has the Catholic Church, the moral majority, and the macho man up in arms against her, but she has also gained the admiration of legions of girls and women, including a new brand of pro-sex feminists, who have discovered in Madonna an ally, a model, a friend, and a sister. No wonder then that some women, like me, started dreaming about her.

In the spring of 1985 I was working on a Ph.D. in folklore studies when I had a dream about Madonna. At that point I had a mild interest in her because my research was on folk Catholicism and I had recently been thinking about feminist interpretations of the Virgin Mary. Just as the image-dominant MTV era was getting started, I was writing about another peak period of image literacy, the High Middle Ages, when the image of *the* Madonna was supreme in Europe and the Virgin

Mary became an overarching visual symbol available for a range of human projections and desires, including female ones. I found it strange that in the late twentieth century once again *a* Madonna was claiming the world's interest. It seemed that both Madonnas succeeded in keeping the attention of their believers through image manipulation, but Madonna Ciccone was a visual symbol invented and reinvented by herself. I was moved by and subsequently dreamed about this woman who carried one of the Virgin's titles, but who, in her advancement of ideas that proclaimed a liberating sexual self-centeredness, seemed bound for a different kind of glory than the Madonna I was studying.

I became increasingly interested in Madonna as a subject of feminist inquiry and inspiration; in fact, I became an expert in Madonna microanalysis and a bit of a guard dog on her behalf. And I continued to dream about her; and on occasion other women I met confessed that they too had dreamed of Madonna. As part of my folklorist's obsession with collecting people's stories, I began my own archive of Madonna-lore, which included a file labeled "Me and Madonna—Dreams." For the most part these dreams were gathered informally, often at parties. When someone told me a Madonna dream, I took down a transcription and threw it in the file. The dreams have been edited minimally here, only for the sake of clarity.

Dreamers represent a range of ages—from thirteen to sixty-one—and locales from across America, Canada, Britain, and France. Clearly many different kinds of women dream about Madonna: a mother, a television producer, a professor, a high-school student, a banker. Some of the dreamers are young, dedicated fans, but most are women in their late twenties to mid-forties who idolize no one. In a *Vanity Fair* interview in 1990 Madonna said, "It's flattering to me that people take the time to analyze me and that I've so infiltrated their psyches that they have to intellectualize my very being. I'd rather be on their minds than off." The range of women whose psyches have been infiltrated by Madonna raises questions about her cultural and personal significance to women. A folklorist leaps on the opportunity to analyze what looks to be the emergence of a new female symbol. Why *do* women dream about Madonna? Does she perhaps, at last, pose the answer to Freud's query, "What do women want?"

Madonna's success has been read in terms of how she resourcefully portrays herself in an unending appropriation of contradictory visual masks and poses. She is the self-anointed queen of image scavenging, of creating identities through a gleeful thievery of appearances. She uses her arsenal of images to do battle with conventional prescriptions that limit her identity in particular and female identity in general.

Madonna *works* that psycho-visual runway: she is mannish, she is girlish, she is virginal; she is whorish, she is Marilyn Monroe, she is James Dean; she is Aphrodite, she is Dionysus, she is whoever she chooses to be; but she is always a woman.

And although one way of explaining the ease with which Madonna unabashedly shifts the presentation of her persona is to call it "taking control" (and this has been the standard media interpretation), another way is to say that these shifts represent a kind of fearlessness. For it is really Madonna's fearlessness that, I think, makes her attractive to women's psyches. In an age when women are attempting to overcome the fear of changing roles, identities, and beliefs, any woman who shamelessly represents the conquest of these fears—and who does so laughingly with tongue in cheek—becomes an excellent candidate for stimulating the unconscious.

For example, I noticed right off that in her first photo shoots and videos (I'm thinking especially of "Burning Up" and "Lucky Star") Madonna began exercising a plucky reversal of the age-old dominance of the heterosexual male gaze. She wasn't just there to be looked at and objectified. She stared back, certain, satisfied, and always drawing the viewer into *her* dominant gaze. Her version of "taking back the night" was taking back the look. Madonna fearlessly insisted on creating a relationship between the viewer and the viewed.

And I think this insistence has played its part in our unconscious reception to her in dreams. Her looking back at us suggested a willingness to know us and to be known.

From the very beginning of her career Madonna opened an invitation to her audience to dream and thereby to choose and to change. In her hit single "Justify My Love" a verse line commands and then asks, "Tell me your dreams. Am I in them?" When Madonna asks if we dream of her, the question seeks an answer because at the heart of her entire project she has urged us to believe that "dreams come true." She constantly uses the phrase as a signature, and it is remarkable that, in her broad articulation of it, such a hackneyed Americanism finds reinvention as a subversive strategy. It seems she intended it that way. Many of Madonna's videos are structured wholly or in part through dream or fantasy. She dreams on the floating bed in "Burning Up," on the bridal bed in "Like a Virgin," on the church pew in "Like a Prayer," and on the beach in "Cherish." Other videos are structured completely as fantasies occupying elaborate dreamscapes: "Express Yourself," "Vogue," "Justify My Love," and "Erotica," where Madonna fully assumes her role as mistress of the dream-like erotic trance. References to the dreamworld emerge in the lyrical content of her songs, including recent works such as "This Used To Be My Playground" and the new song "Waiting" from *Erotica*, in which the listener is asked, "What do I remind you of? Your past, your dreams, or some part of yourself that you just can't love?" One of the texts from *Sex* is told as a dream about lying naked on a beach. In her work Madonna creates a mood that signals her intention to invoke the importance of dreaming and fantasy as methods for designing desire. She is asking us to dream with her, to use dreaming as a kind of discourse—as a language of empowerment, pleasure, and choice. "Dreams come true" is always offered as an invitation. And this invitation to dream is, at the heart, an invitation to own an image of the self. In his "Metapsychological Supplement to the Theory of Dreams" Freud stated, "...dreams are absolutely egoistic and...the person who plays the chief part in their scenes is always to be recognized as the dreamer. We...understand that this is due to the narcissism of sleep." In the narcissism of sleep whatever the dreamer dreams belongs to her. Dreams are about ambivalence and desire; they forward the potential for choice. As the saying goes, "In dreams begin responsibilities...."

Madonna's force, her self-admitted power, rests in large part with her own narcissism, a positive libidinal thrust that admits to a range of ambiguous and fluid personas, each making a claim on the variousness of female identity and eroticism. But whereas the female narcissist generally has been painted by the patriarchy as a nightmare, Madonna once again reverses a trend. Her narcissism is not self-enfolding, negative, or regressive; rather it is offered publicly as a gift, as a source of potential. When Madonna gazes into Narcissus's pool, she sees not one but many images, and through her art she yields them to us for our own self-reflection. Madonna uses a narcissistic strategy to initiate an open dialogue between Self and Other, and keeps it going by refusing to accept the ultimacy of either position. And although there is no easy answer to the question "Who am I?," Madonna implies that there is the possibility of daring to discover the truth of our many selves, a discovery made possible not in dogma but in dreams.

So what is the meaning of women's dreams about Madonna? Certainly no single meaning, but there are themes worth noting. In *Wisdom of the Heart: Working with Women's Dreams* psychologist Karen Signell suggests that women are currently showing new archetypes in their dreams. Signell finds that one such archetype is the sisterly companion, who serves as a helper from the unconscious. Interestingly, women don't seem to dream of Madonna as an unapproachable superstar; rather than viewing her on stage, dreamers often find themselves miraculously transported backstage, where she accepts their admiration or critique on a personal basis.

In fact, the theme that most widely characterizes the dreams in this collection is that of friendship with Madonna. The dreamer realizes that Madonna wants to get to know her or that the two are already friends. Various sub-themes mold the dream narrative of Madonna as sisterly companion: often Madonna introduces a notion of positive self-identity to the dreamer—in effect, she "blesses" the dreamer's desire to accept herself or to realize her potential. In other examples the dreamer must come to Madonna's rescue, sometimes saving her from perilous encounters with sinister men. One woman who dreamed of befriending Madonna actually became her "gal pal" and it is not surprising that she, Sandra Bernhard, crops up often in women's dreams about companionship with Madonna.

And of course it is not unusual that some women experience their dream friendship with Madonna as an erotic encounter. By becoming her lover, dreamers access her erotic power, which Madonna has always claimed as a source of self-knowledge, freedom, creativity, and pleasure. The very essence of the energy that drives the dreaming process is libidinal and erotic. This is no doubt why Madonna has used the dream as an artistic vehicle for revealing her understanding of Eros. And coupled with this understanding is Madonna's project of bringing forth the whole range of women's desires.

If there is one thing she stands for, it is the absence of shame in relation to consensual sexual expression. In fact, it is to her greatest credit that she prefers we interpret her sexuality with the most elastic notion of the erotic that we can muster, especially in the realm of dreams and fantasy. For women, straight or gay, a dream-time rendezvous with Madonna does not reflect the limits of sexual orientation, but instead marks the highest possibility for enjoying the difference that unrestrained erotic pleasure affords.

The radical meaning of friendship with Madonna in dreams is further explained by Jerry Aline Flieger's "The Female Subject: (What) Does Woman Want?" in which she identifies a new symbolic figure, the Prodigal Daughter. Like the biblical Prodigal Son, she abjures paternal control and goes off to experience her own needs and desires, only to return. Unlike the Son, she does not return repentant, but rather "enriched—for she is 'prodigal' in the second sense of the word as well: she is lush, exceptional, extravagant, and affirmative. To be prodigal in this sense is to alter the law, to enlarge its parameters and recast its meaning...." Madonna's biography could easily be cast in terms of the Prodigal Daughter: a woman who left her father's house without his permission, who came to New York to establish her own identity, who became "exceptional" and "extravagant."

In dreams she is the Prodigal Daughter who befriends and encourages other Prodigal Daughters, many of whom, like her, have left the house of the Father.

A number of the dreams occur in a watery environment. Water is charged with the eroticism of sex, birth, and transformation. Women swim with Madonna; they bathe with her; they wade into lakes at her request; and they suffer floods to save her. Water represents a range of unconscious desires, including sexual initiation, purification, and emotional release. Freud summarizes its symbolism in terms of birth and the inevitably problematic unconscious relationship between mother and child. Dreamers often "mother" Madonna—they save her, comfort her, care for her, and so on; and Madonna may be seen to "mother" them by providing a symbolic water for their birth into a new identity. But this mothering relationship is actually based in a sense of sisterly camaraderie and care whereby the affections of mothering are transformed into a ritual of entrustment between two adult women. And although this may seem a most benign kind of affection, it is in fact a radical transgression. Freud asserted the necessity for women to transfer maternal affections to the father, but women's watery dreams of attachment to Madonna harbor the displacement of the masculine as an essential force of definition in the creation of the female self.

Of course, the scariest thing about Madonna from the very beginning was her way of wilfully messing up the male-female categories upon which patriarchy depends. She recasts cultural symbolism in purely female terms, as if everything emanates from the feminine. Madonna the great crotch-grabber and cross-dresser, who shoots her cone tits through a man's suit, becomes Freud's worst nightmare: the phallic woman who does not need to have a dick because she appropriates the idea of having one—in *Sex* she quips, "I have a dick in my brain."

Freud's construction of the female libido was framed absolutely in relation to masculinity. In contrast, Madonna asserts the absolute distinctiveness of the female libido, which is not defined by the masculine, but may in fact absorb it, make use of it, or overtake it—not out of a sense of envy, but rather out of a sense of creativity and knowledge. In *Sex* Madonna herself says, " My pussy is the temple of learning." No wonder then that women affirm their own libidinal autonomy by inviting Madonna into their dreams. In nighttime companionship with her, women know what they want. They want what they want by their own desires. And they want the freedom to express them.

Although the work on this dream collection began some years ago, I find it highly gratifying that publication of the project can now serve as an unofficial response to *Sex*, in which Madonna used a new format to continue the dialogue she initiated early in her career about the importance of dreams and fantasies. And if we think of her project as a testimony to the multi-level pleasures and possibilities inherent in these states, then in many ways this collection is a gift back to her: these dreams represent the other half of the dialogue.

This give and take between Madonna and her female audience is unusual and has unusual implications. In the dialogue between Madonna and her dreamers, dreaming and fantasy are marked as a fluid, private language between women, the effects of which are difficult to control. This libidinal language, based on intuition, feeling, imagery, eroticism, and narcissism, is dangerous to and therefore regularly undervalued, dismissed or censored by the voice of patriarchy. Of course, this is not to say that men don't dream about Madonna: they do. But this project was undertaken with a sense of the unique relationship between Madonna and women; at this point in history it still matters politically and personally that a woman should dare to make her dreams come true. But even more so, Madonna has radically altered the manner by which this fulfilment can be made possible. Women's dreams and fantasies must now be taken into account as a viable means to their own ends, as a way of speaking. What we dream is how we *say* who we might become. In dreaming of Madonna, women dream of unfolding their own desires, they dream that dreams come true.

If Madonna is changing the world—and that would appear to be the case—it is because she signifies the potential for valuing difference that is now possible in the light of a feminist and gay liberation consciousness which she promotes in real ways through her work. As a key symbol of woman's empowerment, she evokes in her many personas political and cultural transformations that have been won in sexual liberation struggles over the past twenty years. And that makes it all the more interesting to discover what women have been dreaming about her. For perhaps someone had to come along who on the world scale of mass culture could represent the shifting power of the masculine to the feminine. The fact that her name happens to be Madonna is an even more intriguing emblem of the move from the dominance of the gods to a revived reign of the goddesses. And that her chosen confirmation name is Veronica ("vera icon" meaning true image) ups the political-symbolic ante of change even further because Madonna actually bears the truth not of a single, but rather of a host of images. And that is where dreams about Madonna play their part in allowing new mythologies of the self to bloom in the dark, uncensored realm of sleep.

I WENT TO A HOUSE VERY MUCH LIKE THE HOUSES ON
Livingston Avenue in New Brunswick, New Jersey. It had two stories,
perhaps three, the third floor being a skylight-type of room. I was
dressed in the long brown coat I used to wear when I roamed those
streets so many years ago in the cold of Jersey's winter.

The house was used by, owned by, or somehow represented a
collective of women with varied feminist goals. As I walked up the
steps I reflected on these women, whom I knew by association only.

My intention was to get to the third floor. No one was there, but
I knew or felt that this was a performance space; it
had the restlessness of a room just vacated after a
happening. I looked out at a wide expanse of night
sky, saw the stars, and felt a sense of wonder. Yet I
had no expectation or clue about what was to come.

In one sudden, miraculous moment Madonna
appeared in and across the wide expanse of night sky.
She was a projection, an apparition, a Madonna in the flesh and in
performance all at the same time. She was the sky, her image filling
up a very large part of the visual space, and she performed in this
sky, which was her stage. She was visible to everyone looking at the
sky at that time.

The effect on me was total. I realized in a great surge of
revelation that this was what we were working toward all this time,
that this was the dimension I had missed: the ultimate performance
art. I had finally understood the deeper meaning of our pop-culture
obsession with the great Madonna.

Nancy, age 39
22 December 1988

23

I'VE ALWAYS WORSHIPPED HER. I REMEMBER WHEN people thought her a ridiculous girl, but she reminded me of myself—of course, I wasn't destined for that kind of fame.

So anyway, I used to have these weird dreams about dancing and acting. You see, I used to perform: I played the piano and went to

acting school. I was living in New York. Not too many people know this, but Madonna used to—before she even sang—she used to do all these off-Broadway things. That's what I was doing. I'd have these dreams that I was dancing, acting, auditioning. And I had this dream that suddenly Madonna appeared and we were auditioning for the same part. Of course, she got the

part, the lead part. But I became her dancer, a secondary role, dancing behind her.

I had this dream a long time ago, the week before her first video came out. I've always loved her. I learned from this dream that I have to keep aspiring. I'm not going to give up. What you do with your talent is the most important thing. She proved that.

Fiona, age 17
16 April 1983

NEW YORK

THE METROPOLIS OF THE WORLD

WE WERE HAVING DINNER AT A FANCY ITALIAN RESTAURANT.
I remember we were seated at a four-person table by the window.
The maitre d' treated us rudely as if we were some low-lifes and
I couldn't figure out why he was being so rude——but we persisted
and were finally seated. Soon after, a rumor began circulating the
restaurant that Madonna was coming and you could feel the
electricity of her arrival. A long white stretch-limo appeared in front
of the restaurant window. The climax of the moment was unbearable.

As Madonna walked into the restaurant I remember
concentrating on her and directing my energy to
attempt to get her to focus on me. But of course I
only looked like a hysterical fan. She walked by me,
indignant, and I knew at that moment that I had
blown it. I was just another common groupie trying to
attract her angelic attentions.

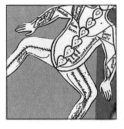

Strangely, it turned out that we had an invitation
to her party, which was being held in a ballroom upstairs. The only
access to it was by elevator. I remember thinking, oh god, here's my
second chance. How can I impress this wóman so she'll pay attention
to me? Up we went, and when the doors opened we saw a group of
people in fancy dress; it seemed like a Jewish wedding. I saw the
bride in her long white gown and then her father. I thought, surely
this can't be Madonna's party, and we proceeded to walk by the
group, heading to the far side of the room. By then I had decided I
was going to get Madonna's attention by wearing a white Italian
straw hat, slanted ever so slightly at a coquettish angle. We
approached Madonna's group; it was small, but the champagne was
flowing in great quantities, and finally the moment arrived. We were

introduced and our glances locked—my dream was coming true. She dedicated her full attention to me and seemed very taken by my dark-haired, handsome look.

Suddenly our clothes were off and she was wrapping her arms around my neck; I put my hands around her hips and her legs around my waist. I was momentarily shocked, but welcomed her advances, although thinking, my god, what's Joanna going to think...oh well, she'll just go with it because she's standing right here—it'll be like a three-way! Madonna began to move her hips in a slow thrusting motion, up and down. I was going out of my mind. I was so excited and happy. I suddenly awoke.

Mary Margaret, age 39
23 September 1990

I JUST REMEMBER ONE IMAGE. AS ALWAYS, I ONLY HAVE one image left. Yes, I'm sitting at the top of a set of stairs——cement stairs, out of doors, schoolhouse steps, urban steps. It's very urban. I'm sitting at the top of the steps with my elbows on my knees, my chin in my hands. You know that position, that position we all know and love. I was very comfortable, comfortable and quietly contemplative. But there were lots of people there, sitting on steps

below me. I think they were all women. We were gathered for some kind of event. There were people on the steps looking down, but there were also people below us sitting on the ground looking up at us. I'm scanning the crowd, checking things out, and my eyes land upon the face of Madonna, sitting down below on the ground with her hands clasped on her knees. She

has a short, blond, rumpled, wet haircut——sort of like she's been swimming or something. Very cute.

As I look at her, she looks at me. She recognizes me. And we just know that we need to get up and leave together. Whatever we are doing there is pleasant, but we need to go. And we get up and leave together. Very satisfying.

Ella, age 32
1 April 1989

NORMALLY WHEN I'VE DREAMT ABOUT HER SHE'S BEEN young and in a strange, weird, unknown location that has the feeling of a maze. I know she's there; I feel her before she arrives. There is always a period of anticipation.

But this time she was older——Madonna as a woman. Like she looks in the "Vogue" video, that kind of make-up, but wilder hair.

 Madonna grows up. Still, this dream had the usual theme of all my dreams about her: some sex, some friendship——that's always the concept. I forget the details; I have dreams about Madonna a lot. I've dreamt about her a thousand times. Would somebody tell her to get the fuck out of my dreams?

It's usually a pick-up scene of some sort. But this one was kind of eerie, I don't know why. There were candles and I pictured her holding a candlestick.

Lynn, age 30
30 January 1991

I HAD A DREAM THAT MADONNA'S REAL NAME WAS BOSWANA.
Everyone who knew her called her that. It's because she's the boss.
That's it.

Mary, age 46
31 December 1990

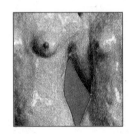

I AM HANGING OUT WITH A BROTHER OF MADONNA'S. He's cute, a John Travolta type, likes music, a little rough. I'm somewhat attracted to him, but the main attraction is his sister sibling. We're in their home (he still lives with Ma and Pa, as does Madonna). He's getting ready to leave and I'm trying to stall in case Madonna arrives. He kisses me and I kiss back. It's very heated at first, but then I start to worry that he's going to want more than I

want to give and that he'll misinterpret my backing off as just using him to get to Madonna, which is not entirely the case. He winds up leaving——on good terms——and I hang out in the house. It's a New Jersey kind of house, an older wood-frame house.

Soon Madonna and Ma come home. We all hit it off right away and start gabbing our guts out—— woman-style, kitchen talk. They show me a back room and describe how they're going to renovate. We discuss every detail.

At one point I make a reference to my weight and Madonna turns to me and says, "Oh Jo, you're so cute," (she's chewing gum as she talks). "You'll look good when you lose weight and all, but you're so cute, that's what you should think about."

Joanna, age 40
16 December 1988

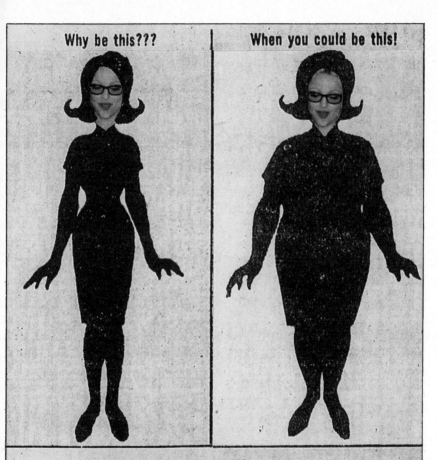

MADONNA AND HER CO-STAR IN "DESPERATELY SEEKING Susan" are staying in a room down the hall. We could be living in a dormitory or camp-type housing. I go in to meet them. It seems that Madonna likes me, is interested in me. When I get up to leave the room, she tells me to stay. I'm probably going to try and find Nancy so that she can meet Madonna, who is really nice.

Paula, age 33
6 April 1985

THERE IS A TOWN I HAVE OFTEN BEEN TO IN MY DREAMS. It's a combination of San Angelo and Odessa, Texas. My grandmother, Ninnie, lives there in a rambling house. She hangs out with Madonna and Sandra Bernhard and thinks that they are fun. She is having them over for dinner and wants me to meet them. I go and watch them all joke and play around in the kitchen. I am getting to see the wild side of Ninnie; they are having such a good time.

Madonna and Sandra live together and work in a frozen chicken factory. They endlessly move lumps of frozen chicken from one place in the factory to another. I hate seeing truckloads of chickens and turkeys going down the highway and am horrified by any business based upon the killing of animals. I can't figure out why Madonna is working there——I didn't think she even ate chicken.

Very soon after I had this dream, several people were killed when a frozen chicken plant exploded.

Janet, age 33
6 February 1991

THERE WAS THIS GOOD-CAUSE GROUP. MADONNA AND
Sean were hosting one of the meetings because they were very
committed members of this organization. In this dream Madonna
lived in the San Remo, the fancy apartment in New York that actually
rejected her application. (She had the last laugh on them in the end.)

So, there were about twenty people seated on folding chairs in
their living room——brown folding chairs——and Madonna gets up
and welcomes everyone and tells them how much she believes in the
cause and how happy she is to have them there. The meeting goes
very well. Everyone thinks she is really impressive. They know she
isn't an idiot and are interested in what she has to say on this
subject. And she is really smart.

Erica, age 35
14 May 1988

THE WORD WAS OUT WITH THE PEOPLE WHO LOVINGLY follow the path of Madonna. A procession at night, a crowd of smiling people, women mostly. She was coming. I was there. More people gathered. We all wanted to celebrate. She moved with all the grace of a body tuned to her temple, to her being—the very soul of her spirit showing as a bright light from her heart and face. We were gathered at the bend. She came dancing, flowing, stretching her arms forward. As she glided past me, I turned and twisted, my feet moving so fast beneath me that I stumbled and fell to the beach. As I picked myself up, my body lurched forward and I craned my neck in search of her. She was ahead as I raced up the sandy hills to catch another glimpse.

Rosemary, age 25
1 November 1990

I DREAMED THAT MADONNA TOUCHED MY NOSE. FREUDIAN implications aside, I knew—in the dream I knew—that no one had touched my nose before. Even though I have made this big deal out of the significance of my nose (the name of my band, endless diatribes concerning my philosophy of smell, etc.), I can't think of anyone who really cared about my nose. Meaning I can't think of anyone who had a natural desire for my nose. These are the feelings of the dream. In the dream itself the touching was very brief, but searching and quite lovely. Madonna's first two fingers felt down from the bump and across the tip.

Kay, age 41
3 November 1990

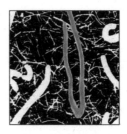

I WAS AT A PARTY AND THERE WAS A NICE ATMOSPHERE. I noticed Madonna through a window in the next room as I was leaving. I tried to connect with her—put my energy out—and when I looked back she looked at me and recognized me. She came outside and said, "Didn't I get a tape from you?" I said, "Yeah" and we talked for a while about it. There were a few other people gathered around, but her attention was all mine. Someone once tried to interrupt and she said, "Will you just wait, I'm talking to Pam." It was great.

Then I saw "Cruela" and her evil sidekick "Tyler" coming up and thought how they ruin everything, but Madonna seemed to recognize "Cruela" and know that she was bad news, so she and I ignored them and continued to talk.

Pam, age 24
10 November 1988

That's weird because I dreamt it last night, but didn't know the interview was on then. That's really weird.

Anyway, in my dream I was in a house and me and my friends (mostly friends from the distant past, college friends, people I hardly  ever dream about) were all sleeping in this room together. My real bedroom was next door with a single bed in it, but I couldn't use it because I knew Madonna was there. Actually, she was prowling around in this corridor outside the room where I was with all my friends. I wanted to sleep in <u>my</u> bed, but I felt she was very lonely and should have it. That was the feeling: that she was excluded; that Madonna would have preferred to have been in with everyone else in the big room.

At one point she was talking with me and I noticed that my robe—sort of a silky dressing gown—was covered in pictures of her, like a pattern, a printed design in pale colors, not very strong. I only noticed this when she pointed to one of my breasts, my right breast, and then I realized her picture was on it.

Vicky, age 36
21 October 1992

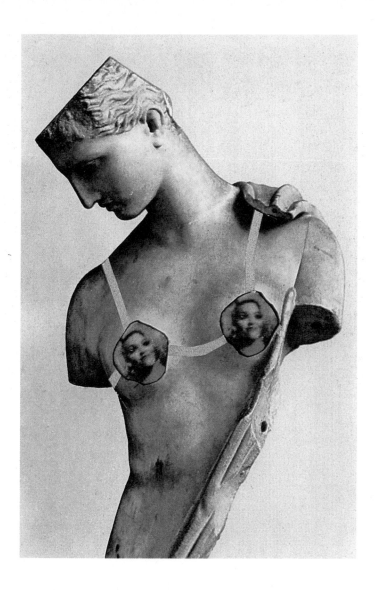

THE SETTING WAS A MUSIC FESTIVAL—WOMEN'S OF COURSE.
I must have been working on the committee or something because I
was all over the place checking on how things were running.

Then I found myself in Madonna's suite of dressing rooms and
in her closet checking out her performance wardrobe: wild, bizarre
clothing with stiff bodices. There was also an assortment of jumpers
of all colors arranged in a rainbow. They reminded me of Catholic
school uniforms. Then there was a big pile (thirty or
so) of pink toothbrushes. There were also a few in the
garbage can, so I figured she must use each
toothbrush only once and then throw it away, but I
didn't ask her that. Actually, I didn't talk to her much
at all. That's all I can remember. Pretty strange.

I told Jan the dream when I first woke up and she
commented that of course I would dream of Madonna considering the
earring I had worn to bed. It's a new earring with a dangling Virgin
Mary medal; it was the first time I had worn it. I was thrilled to have
a Madonna dream, even though the pink toothbrushes make no sense
to me—flamingo pink to be exact.

B.J., age 38
4 April 1992

I AM BROWSING AT A CITY-WIDE GARAGE SALE WHEN
I come upon the "Borderline" Madonna—famous, but not like now—
sitting at a table in the back. It's the end of a long day for her;
business is slow and she is obviously tired. She's friendly in a fake,
distracted way like someone working at a flea market would be.
Since the place is almost deserted, no one is crowding around her or
making a big deal out of her being there, not even me.

I pick up a really gross red plaid coat off her table and think she's
just put a bunch of junk out, nothing really good, when I notice the
$5000 price tag and realize that this is a celebrity fundraiser or
something. She urges me to try on a pair of ugly shorts because I am
obviously the only one there who can fit them. They look awful. But in
an effort to connect with me, she admires what seems to be my
fashion trademark—pink sponge rollers randomly clamped to my hair.
She tells me I look "really raggy" and I know that this is meant as the
highest of compliments.

Allison, age 28
25 September 1991

THE ONE THAT I REMEMBER IN THE MOST DETAIL IS ONE I had when I returned from Los Angeles last fall and we were all consumed with this Madonna/Frida thing. Everywhere we went in L.A. and everywhere you looked—in magazines, in stores, on billboards—was this Madonna/Frida theme.

We met this guy who is the costume designer for a woman doing a Frida Kahlo dance drama and he was aware of Madonna's interest in Frida. He was very excited about her doing a movie about Frida. He had this Frida thing too.

So I dreamt that we were filming the Frida Kahlo movie and Madonna was playing Frida. Lots of my friends were in the movie and my friend Kay was Madonna's right-hand person. Madonna never spoke to anyone directly; she spoke to everyone through Kay. She whispered things to her and then Kay would say, "Well, Madonna said this or that."

We were out to eat and Madonna got upset about something said at the table. Again she spoke to Kay about it, but Kay didn't get mad enough at the group, so Madonna got mad. She was really rude, but we all still loved her anyway.

Rosie, age 29
August 1990

I WAS LYING IN A HUGE EMPTY BED WITH VERY HEAVY blankets over me and I couldn't sleep. I noticed a dim light in the bathroom and got up to see what it was. Standing in the doorway was Madonna, dressed in a floor-length blue velvet robe. She stretched out her arms to embrace me, wrapping her huge robe around us so that I was next to her skin.

She stepped back and I could see that the bathroom was not my own, but rather a much larger version of mine with a big old claw-foot bathtub. There were lighted candles everywhere. The reflections on the tiles and water multiplied the candlelight, making it seem like the room was on fire. Madonna's robe fell to the floor and she guided both of us into the tub. When we sat down the water level came just

under my nipples. We never spoke to each other, but I could hear her voice singing "Like a Prayer."

I thought this was funny and smiled at the humor of it while she poured water from her hands down my forehead. I watched her face as she washed me with a sponge. A halo of golden light appeared behind her head. I unfolded my legs and wrapped them around her while she rinsed my breasts with the warm water. After finishing this ritual she wrapped me in a warm, fluffy towel and led me back to my bed. That glow around her head was still there and as I looked up at it she bent to kiss me and then disappeared.

I felt like I had been baptized by love and sex, that Madonna had somehow cleansed me of past experiences with a violent ex-lover. In the dream I experienced great relief from letting go of these painful memories and I cried with joy from Madonna's gift.

Margie, age 29
14 June 1992

"YOU'RE CURSED by the devil and your soul is destined to burn in Hell!"

Those are the heartrending words of Madonna's dead mom, spoken in a sensational seance July 5.

"Her message was crystal clear," psychic medium Victoria Von Rhome revealed after the exclusive **EXAMINER** seance.

"She told me to tell her daughter: 'You're breaking my heart with your public exhibitions of sex and sacrilege.'"

The chilling communication from Madonna's mom was her first ever since she died 25 years ago. Madonna was only 6 at the time.

"I had tried repeatedly to tune her in, but she remained beyond my ███ until now," said the psy███

"She begged █████████████ her messa███████████ ████ave my dau██████ ███

> Join a unique EXAMINER prayer vigil at noon on Sunday, July 29. We urge all our readers to say a prayer at that time for Madonna's salvation. "My spirit will be w██ you," her mom has prom███

Von Rho██ ████ █████owned clai███ ██████ ███ headlines ██████████cted the recent dev-█████████earthquake in Iran.

She also held the first seance with the spirit of Natalie Wood after the screen star's husband, Robert Wagner, married actress Jill St. John — a story **The EXAMINER** carried exclusively.

Said Von Rhome: "Madonna's shocking displays combining sex with religion have stirred up her mother's spirit terribly. She's asking ███ mom in America for help."

Madonna's mom, for whom ███ ███ was named, is disgusted ███ ██ 31-year-old daughter███ ████ █ni-gans — both o███

The star's ███ ████████ tour feature█████ ███ has her:

● WRIT█████ she rubs her ███ ████exual fa███

SULTRY MADONNA lives ou█ her sexual fantasies in a mag█ azine and on stage (right)█

● **SHOVING HER BREASTS** into the faces of her male back-up dancers while they caress the points of her bra.

● **SIMULATING ORAL SEX** with a guitar player.

● **FONDLING HERSELF** in front of a religious-looking altar o█ burning candles.

● **SMASHING A CRUCIFIX** o█ stage.

● **RAG████████LY** agains█ her fem███ ███████g them t█ █fl███████

███████████almos█

███████s lik█

███████s█

███████p█

███████lle█

███████othe█

███is happe█

███bringing█

███ngs of th█

███from Sea█

███sexual par█

SEANCE SENSATION

90-year███
never too███

EVEN OLDSTERS can ██ shape by pumping iro███ ing to researchers in th█ Of The American Medica██ ciation.

"We placed a group of frail ████

MY MOM IS EVEN GETTING INTO THE GROOVE OVER MADONNA because she had a dream recently that she and I were at one of her concerts together.

She dreamt that we were in this huge concert arena and we were buying thousands of dollars worth of Madonna goodies at this souvenir shop they had there. It had to be a dream because we don't have that kind of money to spend on Madonna stuff, unfortunately. We were going crazy, buying collectible items left and right! While Mom was buying a bunch of Madonna dolls I went ahead to our seats because I didn't want to miss anything. Mom finally stopped buying stuff because the show was  about to start. Our hearts were beating so fast from the excitement and tears were forming in our eyes because we were about to see the greatest and most exciting performer in the whole world! Then, just as Madonna was about to appear on stage, Mom woke up.

What a letdown of a dream, huh? Mom said she wished we could've gotten to see her perform, even though it was only a dream. She woke up too soon and didn't even get to the best part. She wanted to go back to sleep to finish it, but she couldn't. Maybe she'll resume it where she left off some night or, even better, maybe it will come true someday!

Agnes, age 45
20 April 1991

I WENT TO THE GROCERY STORE AND WHILE I WAS IN LINE at the check-out, noticed that Madonna was a few people in front of me. She wasn't an adult though; she was about twelve years old and had a girlfriend with her. I enthusiastically said hello to her and told her that she should come to Roller Towne sometime with me. She thought that would be cool. While I was talking to her I was thinking, how could anyone be offended by this twelve-year-old girl? And it was also very strange to picture her with the ponytail and Gaultier bustier.

Madonna and her friend left the store while I was still in line waiting to pay for my stuff. When I got to my car I noticed that they were across the street at the 200 Club. They still looked twelve. They saw me, waved, and said to come over and hang out with them. I did, but it felt more like babysitting.

Kirsten, age 23
5 September 1991

IT WAS IN THE PARKING LOT OF THE CANADIAN TIRE
store, which sells just about everything but food. The sun was
setting and Raw Bee's Le Gang (the band I was in) were sitting in a
car. Madonna was there in her leather jacket and she had her hair
blond. She was saying goodbye. I remember how happy I felt.
She was smiling at me and then she winked. I smiled and winked
back. She put her hand to her face and smiled. We just looked
at each other without saying anything, then I turned to run.

I missed the green light, so I ran the other way, trying to look
like I knew where I was going. I never looked back——I was going

to cry. I got past the Aylmer Arms building and
stopped on the street right in front of it. I stopped
there and wiped my eyes. I would never tell anyone.

In that dream I had that feeling I often feel,
an almost empty feeling, like there is something very
vital I am missing and longing for. It feels heavy, as
though I've suffered the loss of a loved one. I imagine
that this sadness is something quite similar to what maybe Madonna
felt when she lost her mother.

I imagine that there is a sadness like mine in Madonna. I could
feel it, sort of. In my dream I saw Madonna and I knew that I would
never see her again. But it was going to be enough; I would
remember that moment we exchanged our sadness or whatever it is,
whatever it was.

I remember her with the dim sun's light on her blond hair. It
was really weird. I get this lump in my throat just remembering it.

Lisa, age 17
27 August 1987

WE ARE IN A COLLEGE TOWN GETTING READY FOR MADONNA'S show. Madonna is bossing people about, telling them what to do and saying cutting things to them. It is my job to drive her to the show and make sure she gets there on time.

While in the car we begin making out. I am very nervous, trying to watch for people, keeping an eye out for my girlfriend, who is also around. Kissing Madonna is very strange. When we kiss it feels as though she has very fine gravel in her mouth. So here I am kissing Madonna and it feels like I'm licking a beach.

I drop her off at the show where she is speaking on a panel. I sit next to her on the panel.

Michelle, age 27
July 1991

I WAS IN MY ROOM WHEN MADONNA JUMPED OUT OF one of my posters and "Into the Groove" was playing. We started dancing and laughing and got to be really good friends.

Jeanna, age 13
July 1991

IT'S IN AN AUDITORIUM, NOT A PERFORMANCE SITUATION, but more like Madonna will be speaking for a benefit. Suddenly she is up in the balcony near me. I try to touch her hand and she lets me, then I start talking to her and, to my surprise, she is very nice.

She gets up to go to her dressing room, which is at the back of the balcony. I follow, asking if I can come along. She is talking to me, but I can't understand what she's saying. She goes into her room and closes the door. I press my ear to it and hear her saying something to me that, again, I can't understand. I'm shouting "What? What?" and she opens the door and yells "Chocolate!"

I go back up to where she was sitting in the balcony and there are three packages of different kinds of chocolate candy. I take them to her; she eats some and gives me some. I'm holding an open package and the candy keeps falling out.

She comes out and we are talking and I comment that it's strange but good that she's not getting mobbed. She's dressed in a white terry-cloth robe, like in "Truth or Dare." I wonder to myself if I should ask her about Sandra Bernhard. Finally, I ask her if she has heard of my band and she says she has and that she likes us. I say, "I'm the drummer and we're big fans of yours."

Darby, age 31
7 September 1992

LAST NIGHT I HAD THE WEIRDEST BUT BEST DREAM EVER.
I dreamed that I was doing "Sidewalk Talk" at a school airband
contest. I don't remember who, but I got a boy to do Jellybean's
part, then I did Madonna's part. When the verse came that says,
"When you're living on the street, life can be full of miseries…"
Madonna——I really mean <u>Madonna</u>——came on and started doing it.
I freaked in my dream, but she winked at me and said, like in the
song, "You can do it." So I did finish the song in my fantasy.
She hugged me and said, "Nice going, stranger," like in "Desperately
Seeking Susan." Then I freaked and she said, "Let's talk," and took
my hand and we went backstage. Then I woke up. If that was a
dream, it <u>would</u> be my <u>only</u> dream!

Denise, age 14
11 January 1985

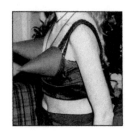

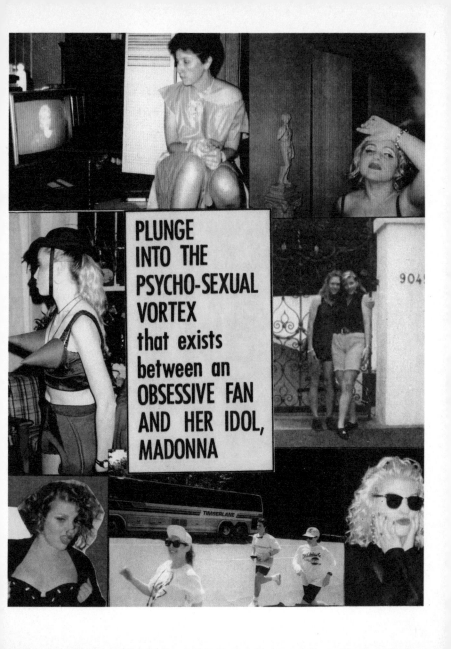

PLUNGE INTO THE PSYCHO-SEXUAL VORTEX that exists between an OBSESSIVE FAN AND HER IDOL, MADONNA

MADONNA APPEARED IN A SENSUAL, LACY BLACK OUTFIT.
She was teasing and capricious and very vibrant. What was up?
Were we going to have sex? She was mysterious and playful.

A bed appeared, the sofabed that my parents have always slept on. Someone was under the sheets. Madonna willed the sheets to lift, just as I was thinking that it was my father and, oh no, I can't see him naked. Well, there he was, and I had that feeling I had as a little girl when I would try to see him when he got out from under the sheets and put on his boxer shorts. I thought my father was

extremely attractive and always wanted to see him naked, especially his penis. There he was, laying out on the bed for me to see. Madonna saw that I was embarrassed, but she didn't try to protect me from my embarrassment/titillation. I was wondering if she was allowing me the opportunity to get turned on to my father and thought for a moment that she might have sex with him, but I reasoned that thought away by equating such an act with incest. Equally, I might have been concerned that I might have sex with him.

Suddenly he was an old man in his seventies, and I focused on his genitals; old and hairless, they lost their potential to arouse me. Madonna had something to do with this transformation. She seemed to be having fun teaching me whatever the lessons were in this situation: basically, that it was alright for me to have all my sexual feelings. They didn't need to be acted on, but should at the very least be acknowledged.

Barbara, age 34
7 July 1991

I HAD A DREAM THAT I WAS ON A SOCCER TEAM AND WE
were in the middle of a big green field with hills all around.
I was standing by a van with a teammate when, from out of
nowhere, Madonna shows up wearing our team uniform. She was
looking at me and talking, but I couldn't hear what she was saying
because I was too busy thinking how strange it was that she was
there on my soccer team acting totally non-famous. I gave her a
puzzled look and walked away.

Lisa, age 25
13 October 1991

I WAS OUT WITH MY MOTHER SOMEWHERE AND WHEN WE came home we saw our house had been robbed. We were both very upset, so naturally we called the police. Well, they said they would send a cop over right away.

A few minutes later there was a knock on the door and I opened it and there she was—Madonna as a policewoman! I already knew that she was a superstar, but apparently she didn't! She just acted like a normal policewoman! She looked very beautiful with her blond hair swept up under her hat. Just as she started to question us about the robbery, I woke up! Oh well, at least I got a chance to see "Sergeant Madonna" at work!

Carol, age 14
May 1990

LOS JÓVENES EN LA JAULA DE LAS MUGERES.

Es tan sagaz la muger,
Y tan débil es el hombre,
Que no es materia que asombre
Jóvenes en jaulas ver:
La gracia, el buen parecer
Cautiva los corazones,
Y sin hacer reflecsiones
Al mirar una beldad,
Quítanos la libertad
La jaula de las pasiones.

THERE WAS A PARADE IN NEW YORK CITY AND MADONNA WAS in it, but for some reason was waiting in the basement of a building.

Apparently she knew me and I told her that Sean was looking for her and wanted to kill her. I said that she shouldn't worry because I'd never let anything happen to her.

Then Sean rushed in with a gun and I turned around and killed him. She said she was sad because she did love him, but that she was most of all relieved because she couldn't go on living with Sean threatening her life every day.

Gwen, age 17
5 July 1987

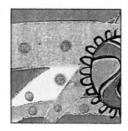

I HAD A DREAM ABOUT MADONNA DURING MY STAY AT
Mill Creek Hospital, which is a psychiatric hospital. No, I'm not
crazy, but at the time I was severely depressed. I am a single parent
of five children and, due to certain incidents that occurred in my life,
I went through a very difficult time coming to terms with reality.
I am an adult survivor of childhood sexual abuse.

In the dream I was in a restaurant with all of my children and
we were sitting there on just your normal average day. In comes
Madonna. She takes a look, not at me but I think at my children.
I guess the children caught her eye, as children can. She was really
friendly, and it was almost as though she wasn't even
a celebrity. She introduced herself and I was so
delighted I didn't hardly know what to say. She
chatted for a while with the kids and I mentioned
that I wrote to her about the problem of sexual
abuse. She was interested in this issue and very
interested in helping in any way she could. It was
great. She wanted to hear what it was like and how a message about
this problem could penetrate society in a controversial way so
people would pay attention.

After talking, she thanked me for introducing my children to her
and of course I was surprised. I felt so honored and fortunate, it
blew me away. And that's that. It was a really neat dream and it
came to me at a time when I was really going through a lot of
emotional turmoil, so it felt like magic almost.

Chris, age 35
13 February 1991

ycy sont ceulx celles . qui ow
fait le psaultic

Reneé·91

I WAS AT A MADONNA CONCERT WHICH WAS BEING HELD in a small amphitheatre. My really religious sister, Mary, was with me, so I was kind of nervous as to how she would see the show or if she would be offended.

Madonna was wearing a blue granny-style bathing suit and doing a lot of funny moves, which made me laugh, nudge my sister, and tell her the names that I had made up for those moves, such as "The Bowling Move."

After Madonna's performance other performances were scheduled, so she sat down in one of the amphitheatre seats. I immediately jammed over to where she was and sat in the seat next to her. We started talking and found out that we had a lot in common, and she began to drag me all over the place, yanking on my arm and introducing me to all  of her friends. Then she began to take me all over town with her because she had a lot of social appointments that night. We went to all these places and just totally talked dish to each other about everyone, laughing at how pretentious they all were.

Finally morning came and it was time for her to take me home. She pulled up to my house and gave me a hug and a kiss goodbye. Then she grabbed both of my hands and said, "I have something for you." She pressed a key into my hand and said, "It's the key to Sean Penn's house. He's up there waiting for you right now." I thanked her ecstatically and hugged her goodbye.

Margaret, age 20
23 August 1991

I WAS SITTING ON TOP OF SOMEONE'S STOMACH. IT WAS all cozy around us, like we were in a closet or a small, enclosed warm space, almost like a bathtub. The person and I were making love. I looked down at the body under me and it was Madonna. I remember being amazed that it was Madonna, but it felt perfectly natural. I looked at her body a lot and remember some straps or clothing with holes in it, but they were all symmetrical, not random.

Zizi, age 33
11 September 1991

I WENT TO CALIFORNIA TO VISIT AND I SOMEHOW ENDED UP hanging out with Madonna in her new four-story castle. She was bored and didn't seem real happy and she and I and about ten other people would pile into her little Mercedes 350SL and drive on these winding, mountainous roads. She would very dryly say things like, "Yeah, this is safe."

Suddenly we were in Seattle, about to get something to eat, and Madonna disappeared, but told my friend that she would meet us later.

k.d. was in town, so I called her to meet me. She came to a party at my friend's house. When she arrived I was outside, but when I walked towards her to greet her, Melissa was walking up with her girlfriend and her girlfriend nudged me out of the way and said, "You know how it is" and walked away with k.d. They were stars, I was not, and I needed to move aside. I tried to talk to k.d. again at the party and later called her where she was staying. She was cold to me and my feelings were hurt.

I was also upset because Madonna didn't call or show up again. She drank two cups of something a day and had already had one, and this was somehow a reason why she didn't follow through on her dinner plans with me.

Jan, age 35
8 January 1993

I WAS HANGING ON THE EDGE OF A CLIFF WATCHING
the Red Hot Chili Peppers shoot their new video. I tried to lift myself
up on to the cliff, but it was too hard. Then some guy helped me up.
It was one of the guys from Living Colour. I told him that I saw his
band and that they were really great. He was passive about it all,
so I walked away and I went over to this booth.

Inside, they were showing a movie where Madonna was playing
an acrobat. She was wearing a pink bodysuit and was hanging from a
trapeze bar, being very funny. Then Madonna herself peeked into the

booth. She looked at me and then the movie, smiled
and walked next door to her private tent. I followed
her in there and we both started talking about getting
away and I said, "Haven't you read any of the
fantasies I sent you?" and told her about riding horses
in a meadow, eating chocolate, and reading "The
Great Gatsby." She said, "'The Great Gatsby' is such a
wild book." I agreed and said that I knew of many great, dishy
books that we could read. Then her "Lucky Star" video came on the
television. I was glad, but Madonna turned it off.

Then a little girl came in and she was sad because she was
eating a brownie with butter, but the last piece of butter had
ketchup on it. She wanted to open a new stick, but her mother made
her use the piece with ketchup. Madonna and I said that if we were
her mother we would have let her open up a new stick of butter and
save the ketchup butter for something more appropriate.

Kirsten, age 23
3 August 1991

BASICALLY, I WAS GOING SHOPPING WITH MADONNA

and my mother. I was looking for a wedding dress and slips for it. I was looking for something 1950s style, real tight in the bodice. I was in the dressing room with Madonna and I had this feeling that my mother didn't like her. She didn't say anything, but we know our mothers. I knew she didn't like her and it wasn't comfortable.

There was also something else going on: some gangsters were after Madonna. I was in a new atmosphere, a mixture of Manhattan and downtown L.A., on a kind of rainy day. And we were running from dressing room to dressing room trying to get away from these guys. And the slips—I didn't like the way any of them looked on me.

Roxanne, age 35
13 November 1992

EMBLEMS OF THE DISTRACTED TIMES, 1642.

And sure this is a Monster of strange fashion

I WAS SWIMMING IN THE OCEAN WITH SOME FRIENDS. We were out far enough so the water was up to our necks. I saw Madonna swimming in the distance and I tried to reach her, but she disappeared.

Later in the dream I told a friend that I'd seen Madonna and that I really wanted to tell her that I'd been dreaming of swimming with her. My friend asked if I knew the significance of water in dreams. I answered, "Sure, sex."

The next day I was back in the water and I saw Madonna again. This time she swam toward me and I told her about my dreams. She laughed and we talked as we swam to the shore.

Suddenly we were dry and dressed. She grabbed my hand and pulled me after her as she ran toward town. I was aware that I was giving in to her, that she was taking me somewhere I'd never been.

We walked on dirt paths through a village of gypsies and circus people. We stopped to watch a man in a white suit prepare for his nightclub act in a tent. He had a curtain of champagne glasses that he was strumming and tuning as he rehearsed. Madonna laughed so hard she doubled over.

We stopped to eat and drink in another tent. There was music everywhere and we danced all along the way. No one spoke to us.

Eventually, we got to this dirty, run-down hotel. She pulled me into an elevator where there was a fat man with a moustache. I held on to her because the elevator lurched. I was scared. The doors finally opened and we had to crawl up on to the hallway. The next thing I knew, I woke up naked in bed, not sure of what had happened. I got up and wrapped a sheet around me. It was morning and the sun was just rising. The room was warm.

From the window I could see Madonna sitting on the beach with her back toward me, her knees drawn up to her chest. She had on a loose white shirt with red polka dots and her blond hair was moving in the wind. She was looking out to sea. There was no one else in sight. As I watched her, she turned her head toward me, as if she felt me there. She smiled——a flirting, sheepish face. I was thrilled.

Liz, age 29
5 July 1991

IN MY DREAM I WAS TRYING TO MAKE LOVE TO MY PARTNER, but she was being fussy and unresponsive. This irritated me, so I pulled away and as I did I looked over and saw not one, but five Madonnas all dressed identically in black teddies and fishnet stockings. They were having a huge orgy that seemed very fun and inviting. I joined in enthusiastically. Then I had an orgasm that woke me up.

Beth, age 26
28 November 1992

THE FIRST PART OF MY MADONNA DREAM TOOK PLACE IN A large dressing room. A girl named Tammy—who used to be with me in a vocal group—and I were trying on different clothes to get ready to go on stage with Madonna. It was sort of an audition for us to be her back-up singers. I don't remember much about being on stage, but later Tammy and I were walking down a sidewalk and Madonna was coming up the sidewalk on the opposite side of the street. When we saw each other Madonna indicated that she wanted to work with Tammy. Then she said to me, "You don't have enough spunk."

Kaye, age 29
1989

CAREER GIRL

A girl trying to decide between a career or ma... bewildering problems. These GUIDES offer expli... information on nearly every phase of settling ...nd a new lif...

- [ ] CHECK LIST FOR DECISION: CAREER, COLLEGE OR MARRIAGE ....(25¢)
- [ ] 25 KEYS TO MEETING PEOPLE AND MAKING FRIENDS ....(25¢)
- [ ] COLLEGE AT NIGHT: SHORTCUT TO PERSONAL SUCCESS ....(25¢)
- [ ] HOW TO BRING OUT YOUR "HIDDEN BEAUTY" (incl. 15 Glamour Secrets of Top Models) ....(25¢)
- [ ] HOW TO BREAK INTO TELEVISION ....(25¢)
- [ ] HOW TO BREAK INTO SHOW BUSINESS/THEATRE (25¢)
- [ ] HOW TO BREAK INTO MODELING ....(25¢)
- [ ] HOW TO BECOM... LINE H...

- [ ] HOW TO LAND A JOB I... ADVERTISING/PUBLICIT...
- [ ] HOW TO BECOM... SALARY EXECU... RETARY
- [ ] HOW TO BR... ION EXE... ER/BUYE...
- [ ] WARDRO... HA... LO...
- [ ] DAT... TIN... TO...
- [ ] REL... CR...

- ...OVE TO NEW YO...
- ...O FIND A JOB ...YORK ....
- ...TO FIND AN A... ...ON A BUDGET ...ALONE vs ...IARING
- ...DECOR... ...NT O...
- ...IDE T... ...INEX... ...I TO F... ...OUND
- ...RE ...O M... ...R TO M...KE ...K ...C AND MEET PEC...LE ...OU OWN AGE ....(25...
- [ ] COMPLETE LISTING O... OVER 400 ADDITIONA... SELF - IMPROVEMENT CA... REER GIRL GUIDES ...(25¢)

Cho... ...; sen... the... ...CIAL: Any 5 mailed to you for only ... For only $2.00. P... ...livery. Enclose Coin, Money Order o... ...: On orders under 5 books ...xtra for postage and handling.

...ONEY BAC...

CAR... ...IRL GUIDES, Dept... ...t., New York, N...

I enc... ...If I h... ...nly $1.00. I... have checked 11 ite... ...e f...

Name _____

Address _____

City _____State_____

MADONNA GIVES A CONCERT IN A VERY TINY SPACE THAT has a huge domed ceiling under which are stacked vertical rows of seats. Soon she performs again and I assist her for the last number. She's doing a special voice-over to "Vogue," the record of which she puts on the large turntable she's brought. I go up to her afterwards to where she sits behind a table, which keeps moving backwards — perhaps I am leaning too far forward in my eagerness to talk.

We retreat to an alcove off to the side. I tell her of my excitement at her ability to condense her songs to a single phrase

that then translates to a single video image. She is excited about this, agreeing with me vigorously.

Then I talk to her about Kay, who hasn't yet arrived, and explain the altarmaking projects. She is somewhat sceptical at first, but as I continue to explain, suddenly catches on. Madonna explains to me that the silver bracelets she's wearing are her own private project, that they are not meant to withstand wear and tear, but are special visual objects. I wake up convinced that she is intelligent and friendly.

Ann, age 33
7 May 1991

I WAS DATING A WRITER FROM "VANITY FAIR." GORGEOUS, kind of upstanding, from a family like the Kennedys—he seemed very JFK, Jr.

Madonna was coming over to my house to visit us. She came in the front gate of my apartment building and thought the whole thing was my place. She started knocking on people's doors,

thinking they were different bedrooms in my house, looking for me. When she got to my apartment I opened the door, and all of a sudden my apartment was huge—all these different rooms with only three walls, like stage sets, sprawling all over the place.

We walked through the rooms, which were all crooked and kind of rickety, until we came to a big, airy space. I sat next to my boyfriend on this old, ripped-up Victorian couch, and Madonna sat in an old velvet chair.

I start talking real filthy, and my boyfriend looks at me and says, "My God, were you raised by a sailor?" All of a sudden Madonna says, "No, she was raised by me," and we both break out into conspiratorial laughter. I woke up laughing.

Molly, age 27
29 November 1992

A COUPLE NIGHTS AGO I DREAMED THAT MADONNA WAS in town and staying at my house. She let it be known that she was looking for me—she had heard that I was a hot ticket—and I let it be known that I wanted her.

The house had communal showers, like a dorm, and I went to them when I knew she'd be there. There were several people around in the shower area, including one of my brothers.

Madonna was getting out of the shower just as I was getting in the one next to hers. As she leaned down to pick up a towel she met

my eyes with desire. She lowered her blackened lashes and her full breasts pressed together briefly and then were covered by the towel. She was very casual, oblivious to the other bathers in the room. There was an unknown man standing behind me.

I looked at Madonna with lust and she was coy. Snubbed by her nonchalance I said, "Send in any guy with a cute butt," and then got into the shower. The unknown man got in shortly after that. We embraced, and I knew it was Madonna, but her _male_ energy. We stood under the stream of water, letting it run down his chest hair and between my breasts, sliding off the sides of our bellies where our bodies were pressed together. She said, "You have a great body. In your own way you're as built as I am."

When I held her I realized she felt like my lover Carol. Her energy, I mean. It was like all other appearances were a mask.

Cheryl, age 29
28 March 1991

KIRSTEN, TRISTAN AND I WERE AT A MADONNA CONCERT.
For some reason there was a major flood and everyone started freaking out and running for the doors. Madonna was doing her show from a tower, and she became trapped at the top of this tower as the water rose higher and higher. No one thought about going up to aid her except Kirsten and me.

She was leaning over the edge just watching the water rise. As she saw us approaching she began to look very apprehensive, but

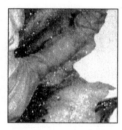

I just went up to her and said, "Would you like us to help you get out of here?" She nodded, so I took off my sweatshirt and said, "Put this on and the hood over your hair so no one will recognize you." Then I handed Tristan to her and told her to hold him because no one would expect Madonna to exit her concert holding a baby. Also, I told her to kind of hold him in front of her face, but she didn't listen to me and held him down by her stomach, so her face was still visible. However, we were able to pass through the hallways without her being recognized. Then Kirsten and I gave her a ride home.

Margaret, age 19
24 April 1990

I WAS IN BED, NAKED PERHAPS, AND MAD AT MADONNA—
why, I have no idea. I was pouting when she came into the room. It
was her body alright and she was talking excitedly about her
performance. Something about how she had to get into a certain
position so she could sing her best. Arching back into the pose, her
nipples grew erect. Next thing you know, she and I were rolling
around, and I have a very vivid memory of staring into her genitals.

Pamela, age 29
26 September 1992

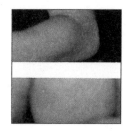

IN MY DREAM I WHO IN NON-DREAM LIFE HAVE DARK auburn hair had platinum hair done in a bob, just below my chin and turned under. Also, I was wearing a black beret tilted at a jaunty angle and my lips had dark red lipstick on them. As I was taking in this alien image of myself in the mirror I realized with a start that I looked just like Madonna looking like Dietrich or Garbo—the great blond faces of the twentieth century.

Carol, age 40
11 November 1992

I AM AT MADONNA'S APARTMENT WITH HER AND OTHERS. She takes an interest in me and I take her aside and draw her out as a deep and serious person. We have the most wonderful talk. She serves me coffee, then tops it with a dollop of mashed potatoes—silly girl.

She takes a spoonful from my cup, eats it, then scoops out the remaining potatoes and replaces them with whipped cream. I see her later the same night at a function of some sort. I approach her in the ladies room and introduce myself, "Hi, remember me, the teacher?" She looks straight through me with no recognition.

Donna, age 46
16 September 1992

WONDE'S
TUTTIMINT
SNAPPY GUM
BE ALWAYS HAPPY WITH PRACTICAL JOKE

I AM WALKING DOWN A PATH WHICH CROSSES OVER
a shallow stream via a footbridge. Madonna is sitting on a large rock
in the middle of this stream. She has a forlorn look on her face.
I approach her through the stream and say, "I've been looking for
you everywhere. Let me take you away from all this." And after
taking her hand I pull her up and she buries her head just above my
breasts. We remain there for what seems an eternity, mostly in
silence, with my arms sheltering her, until she stands up, kisses me
tenderly on the lips, and walks away.

Monica, age 27
3 November 1991

I WASN'T SURE EXACTLY WHAT TO DO AS I WANDERED through the studio. Madonna had called and asked that I stay with her awhile. She was lonely and just wanted people around her. "Bring your friend Steve, too," she'd said. Steve and I were now in Madonna's art studio with its tall ceilings and broad open space. The cement floor made the room seem cool and comfortable. Large canvases on easels were shrouded with plastic and scattered across the expanse of the room.

In the very center of the room, in the middle of a patch of sunlight, Madonna sat on a tall stool working on a painting. The canvas was huge, about 6x5 feet. I couldn't see what she was painting, even when I walked to the side of the canvas, but she was using oil paint; I could easily see that from my position. With a grey beret on her head and a dark artist's smock over her jeans she looked perfectly in tune with her work.

Madonna had said she didn't want people around always talking to her; she just wanted people nearby. That's why she'd thought of me, she said.

Steve was investigating a corner of the studio, so I decided to look around. We hadn't seen the rest of the house, but I knew it was huge and that the large ornate escalator near one end of the studio would take us up to our rooms. I wasn't yet ready to see the upstairs, so I walked past the escalator and found myself facing a wall with a large doorway cut into it. This doorway led directly into a supermarket. How strange, I thought, as I passed into the store.

There were many shoppers, but none of them seemed to see the passage into Madonna's art studio. In fact, none of them seemed to realize that the store they were in was a portion of Madonna's home.

I laughed quietly to myself as I walked the aisles, watching old women carefully choosing canned goods, young mothers running harried through the store, and attractive young adults cruising each other near the produce.

I walked back through the doorway and told Steve, "There's a whole store out there!" Madonna glanced up from her work and smiled at me briefly before turning her attention back to the painting. It was time, I decided, to see the rest of the house...

Kim, age 24
April, 1992

"It's flattering to me that people take the time to analyze me and that I've so infiltrated their psyches that they have to intellectualize my very being. i'd rather be on their minds than off."

I WOKE UP SOMETIME DURING THE NIGHT AND DECIDED TO stay up since I wasn't tired. I thought I might go outside for some air.

I looked at myself in the mirror and discovered that I was very unattractive: my hair was in rubber rollers with plastic pins poking out everywhere and my bathrobe was old and dingy—a sort of off-pink color. My feet were held hostage by my brown slippers,

which are decorated with blue polka dots. Well, I was pretty disgusted with my appearance, but I headed out my back door assuming no one would see me in such a state.

As I opened the door I saw that my backyard had completely vanished; in its place was a large room where a group of people were seated around a table. I was curious, so I casually walked over to them. To my great surprise I recognized one of the people sitting there. It was Madonna. I was stunned. She and her friends were chatting away, very involved in their conversation. Her friends were all dressed nicely, but she still stood out. Her hair and make-up were perfect in every way. She wore a gray pin-striped skirt and matching blazer, kind of a business suit, with high black heels and sheer stockings. She looked exquisite and she knew it.

Suddenly she noticed me standing there staring at her. She looked at me as if I were from outer space and began to examine me, her eyes moving up and down. Then she said with a sneer, "Ugh, what a mess!" I was so embarrassed. I tried to fix my hair.

Eleanor, age 61
7 February 1993

WELL, IN THIS DREAM I WAS ON A DATE WITH MADONNA. That may sound strange, but in the dream I was a guy, which <u>is</u> strange because I'm a girl. I know that makes no sense whatsoever, but I'll continue anyway.

We were in my basement, which then turned into a giant highway. We were driving a motorcycle with no motor; I guess you could call it a cycle. Then we passed a lake on the side of the road with little baby sheep swimming around in it. Madonna wanted me to get her one, so I waded into the water and looked for the cutest little baby sheep I could find. I chose one, picked it up, and handed it to her. Then we decided it would be best to let it go, so I pushed it toward the others, which were already swimming away. We stood there together and watched them swim until they were out of sight.

Renee, age 18
20 April 1991

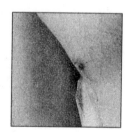

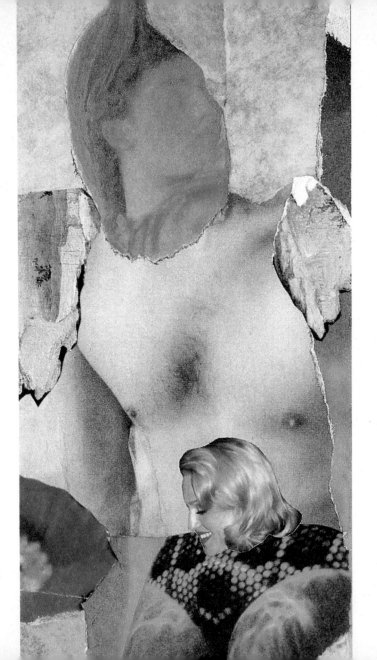

I DREAMED THIS MORNING THAT I WENT TO SEE ROXANNE to do an interview for her TV show. She was doing a special on Madonna and asked me to serve as an expert on the subject. I went to her apartment. It was full of light and very spare, almost austere, but quite peaceful. Roxanne greeted me wearing a loose green gown with little flecks of gold in it. Over her head she had on a blue cowl-like hood. I could hardly see her face, but I sensed that she was quite beautiful. We sat down and began to talk about Madonna. For some reason, though, I began to feel extremely nervous. I started to have this realization that Roxanne was dressed as the Virgin of Guadalupe or that she was the Virgin of Guadalupe! It blew me away. My nervousness increased drastically. I couldn't imagine what I would say to the Virgin about Madonna  and was having a physical reaction, shaking and tongue-tied. Then Roxanne left the room and came back momentarily to offer me a drink. It was in a little plastic cup, kind of like a medicine cup. I wasn't sure I wanted to take it. She held it up to me and said, "This is something called 'mother's milk.'" That really made me nervous. I hesitated, but I did drink it. It was a cream liquor that tasted like Bailey's. I felt better.

Kay, age 44
10 November 1992

Special "Live To Tell" thanks go to Miss Mary, Deano, D.M.C.O., Cherese, Denise, De Mark, Dr. Ann, Lynn, Janet, Ricki, Dr. Ed, Ella, Post, Rosemary, Patty J., Manuela, Cynthia R., Mary Margie, Martha B., †Michael W.†, Peggy V., B.V.M., Mom, Tia, and Girls in the Nose.

Credits: Madonna image / other graphic elements. Page numbers are in bold.

1 Oliviu Savu / 19th-century engraving after a 16th-century miniature by Giulio Clovio representing Dante and Beatrice transported to the moon, from "Il Paradiso." **2** Renee Polgar. **4** Renee Polgar. **5** Oliviu Savu / Early 20th-century German print. **7** Courtesy of Rosewick / engraving, "Eclipse of the Sun," from *The Pictorial Press* by Mason Jackson, London 1885. **22** Michael Ferguson, Globe Photos / "Venus," Lucas Cranach; photo of the planet Venus, NASA. **25** Eric Watson, Star File / 1930s postcard. **26** Daniel Simon, Gamma Liaison / various figures from copyright-free and other sources, "Vaginal Pride" concept from WHAM. **29** Oliviu Savu / Polaroid photograph by This Dream Team. **31** Oliviu Savu / 1960s postcard. **33** Frank Schramm / *Medusa* (Lynn Keller) by Kris Johnson. **35** A. Berliner, Gamma Liaison / Nefertiti; "Le Due Sorelle," terracotta sculpture by G. Chessa, 1930s. **37** Oliviu Savu / 1960s advertisement. **39** Philippe Duprat, Gamma Liaison / promotional postcard for El Patio Motel, Spur, Texas. **41** David Bennett, Gamma Liaison / promotional postcard; marbled paper. **42** Oliviu Savu / Ella Gant. **45** Oliviu Savu / yard shrine in San Antonio, Texas, photo by Kathy Vargas. **47** Oliviu Savu / courtesy of Girls in the Nose, Kay Turner, Daphne Shuttleworth. **49** Oliviu Savu / print after the painting *Expectation* by Meyer von Bremen, late 19th century. **51** Lorraine Kelly, hand-tinted by Sister Buzz / Aphrodite of Capua, Naples. **52** Oliviu Savu / toothbrush watercolor by B.J. Ryan; gouache painting of traditional Belgian folk figure, Nanesse. **55** Oliviu Savu / 19th-century electrotype of Egyptian ornaments, early 20th-century Japanese wrapping paper. **57** Courtesy of Rosewick / 19th-century engraving after a painting of St. Ursula by Hans Memling; rendering by Margie Lawler of *My Birth* by Frida Kahlo. **59** Oliviu Savu / pastel by Margie Lawler. **60** Oliviu Savu / "Seance Sensation," courtesy *The National Examiner*; clown stamp; holy cards of the Virgin of Guadalupe, and Anima Bendita. **63** Oliviu Savu / Dutch 19th-century chromolithographic trade card. **65** Oliviu Savu / detail from Giotto's frescoes from *The Life of St. Francis*. **67** Peggy Moffitt and Madonna by Lise Rose, Globe Photos / 19th-century French chromolithograph after an illuminated manuscript. **69** Oliviu Savu / drawing by Diane Di Massa, courtesy of Giant Ass Publishing, New Haven, Connecticut. **70** T. McGough, Gamma Liaison / NASA photo of the Martian landscape by the Viking Lander Imaging Team; 16th-century German woodcut. **73** captioning from a poster for "Fan Mail" performed by Nancy Swartz, fan photos courtesy of Madonna Maniacs. (Madonna is the right-hand figure in the jogging photo.) **75** Oliviu Savu / "breasts" fashioned by K.T. from Indian printed paper. **77** Werb, Gamma Liaison / 1930s wallpaper. **79** Oliviu Savu / 19th-century Spanish broadside of a folk ballad; cat from a 1930s French postcard. **81** Oliviu Savu / early 20th-century Japanese wrapping paper; hair "dizzled" by Sister Buzz. **83** Oliviu Savu / collages by Sheri Tornatore. **85** Renee Polgar / 19th-century chromolithograph. **87** Luc Novovitch, Gamma Liaison (still photo from "Justify My Love" video) / anonymous Polaroid photograph of salt and pepper shakers. **89** A. Berliner, Gamma Liaison / anonymous 1960s magazine photo; First Communion snapshot, anonymous photographer, 1930s. **91** Oliviu Savu / Pompeiian fresco, drawing by Janet Redwine. **93** Oliviu Savu / 17th-century engraving from *The Pictorial Press*, Mason Jackson, London, 1885. **94** Tony Savino, Gamma Liaison / early 20th-century postcard. **97** Oliviu Savu / Madonna Road photograph by Celeste Tibbetts. **99** Lorraine Kelly / photograph by Kent Loving, courtesy of Lauren Sommer. **101** Crayola drawing by Susan Greenfield / 1960s advertisement. **103** Bennett-Spooner, Gamma Liaison / late 19th-century chromolithograph; gouache painting of traditional Belgian folk figure, Nanesse. **105** Renee Polgar / collage by Sheri Tornatore. **107** Oliviu Savu / 19th-century steel engraving after a Greek vase. **109** T. McGough, Gamma Liaison / anonymous Polaroid photograph. **111** Oliviu Savu (center) / photos from the "Pomegranate Series" by Dixie Sheridan. **113** Oliviu Savu / hand-tinted photograph by D.S. Field, circa 1930. **115** Oliviu Savu / 20th-century practical joke novelty. **117** Oliviu Savu / 19th-century photograph, photographer unknown; 19th-century chromolithograph. **119** Oliviu Savu / 16th-century German woodcut majuscule, glamorized by Sister Buzz. **121** Oliviu Savu / 1930s advertisement; quote from Madonna: *Vanity Fair*, April 1990. **123** Oliviu Savu / anonymous "whoopee cushion" drawing, circa 1930s. **125** Oliviu Savu / collage by Sheri Tornatore. **126** Oliviu Savu / multiple Virgins; buttons courtesy of Kolwyck-Turner Productions, all rights reserved.